Quickly's Safari Adventure
Coloring & Activity Book

S4S

Dancing Mommy Press

Miriam Kronish and Jeryl Abelmann
Illustrated by Daniel J. Seward

Quickly's Safari Adventure Coloring & Activity Book

Copyright © 2016 by Jeryl Abelmann & Miriam Kronish

For information or to order additional copies please contact:

Dancing Mommy Press
P.O. Box 321
Pebble Beach, CA 93953

www.DancingMommyPress.com

Designed and illustrated by Daniel J. Seward.

Visit us on the Web:
www.QuicklyTheMagicSpatula.com
www.SisForSafari.com

ISBN: 978-0-9971084-9-1

Printed in the USA
2 4 6 8 9 7 5 3 1
First edition

QUICKLY'S
Safari Adventure

Color your way through a South African safari
with Quickly and his friends.

Let's start with a Pancake Cookout!

Crack QUICKLY's Code

A	B	C	D	E	F	G	H	I
1	2	3	4	5	6	7	8	9

J	K	L	M	N	O	P	Q	R
10	11	12	13	14	15	16	17	18

S	T	U	V	W	X	Y	Z
19	20	21	22	23	24	25	26

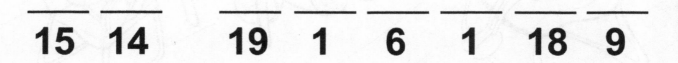

__ __ __ __ ,
23 5 18 5

__ __ __ __ __
7 15 9 14 7

__ __   __ __ __ __ __ __
15 14   19 1 6 1 18 9

Antelope

Buffalo

Cheetah

Dragonfly

Elephant

Flamingo

Giraffe

Hippopotamus

Impala

Jackal

Klipspringer

Lion and Leopard

Monkey

Nagapie

Ostrich

Penguin

QUICKLY

Rhinoceros

Safari

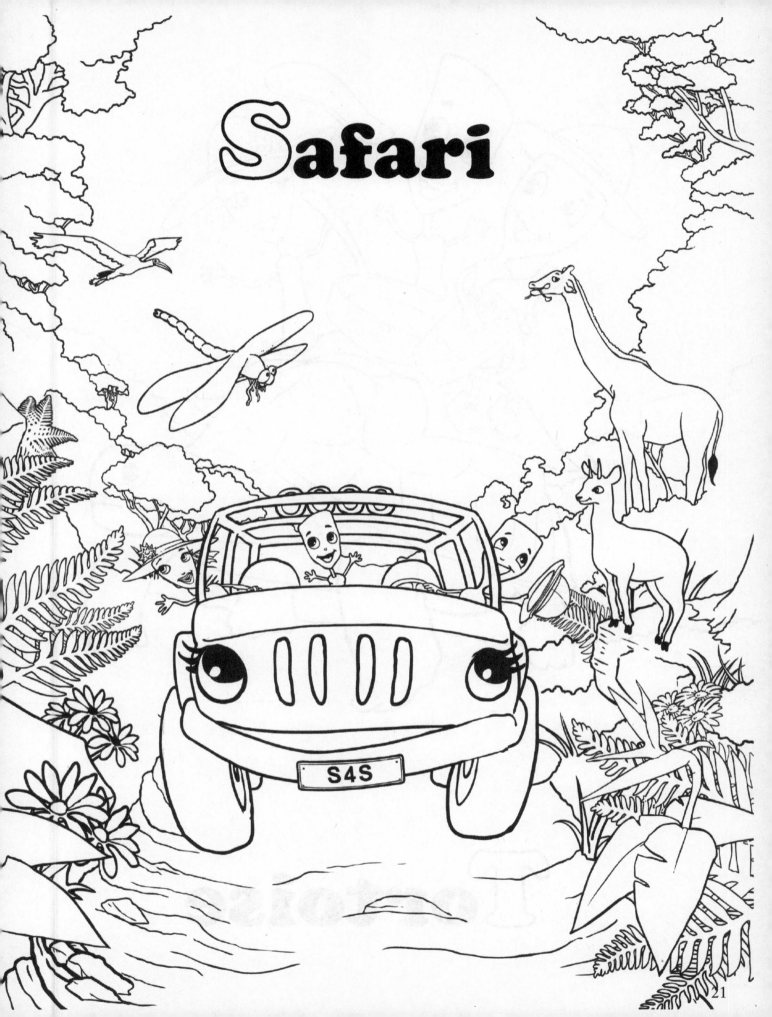

Tortoise

Umbrella Tree

Victoria Falls

Warthog

Xhosa

Yellow-billed Stork

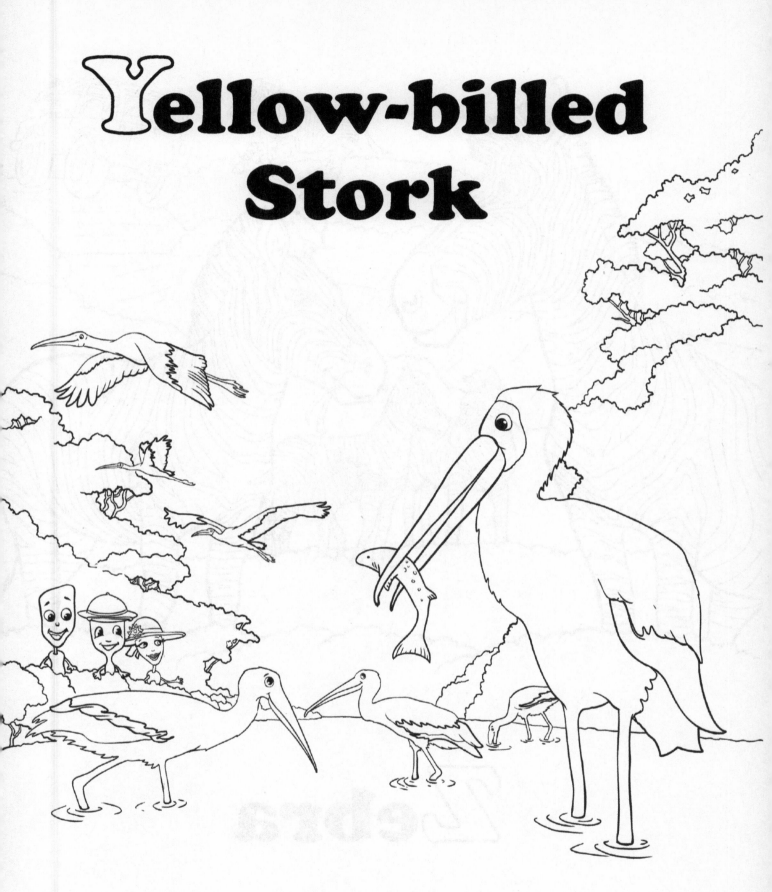

Zebra

Fun With

QUICKLY

THE MAGIC SPATULA

and his friends

Ponnie   QUICKLY   PanDora

Help QUICKLY find his pancakes!

START

FINISH

Draw your favorite pancakes for **QUICKLY**.

Happy Pancaking!

There are 21 Quicklys hiding in the kitchen.
Circle all the Quicklys you can find.

Color all the flowers.

QUICKLY's Shadow Play

Match each shadow to its character.

Find what's different.
Make them all the same.

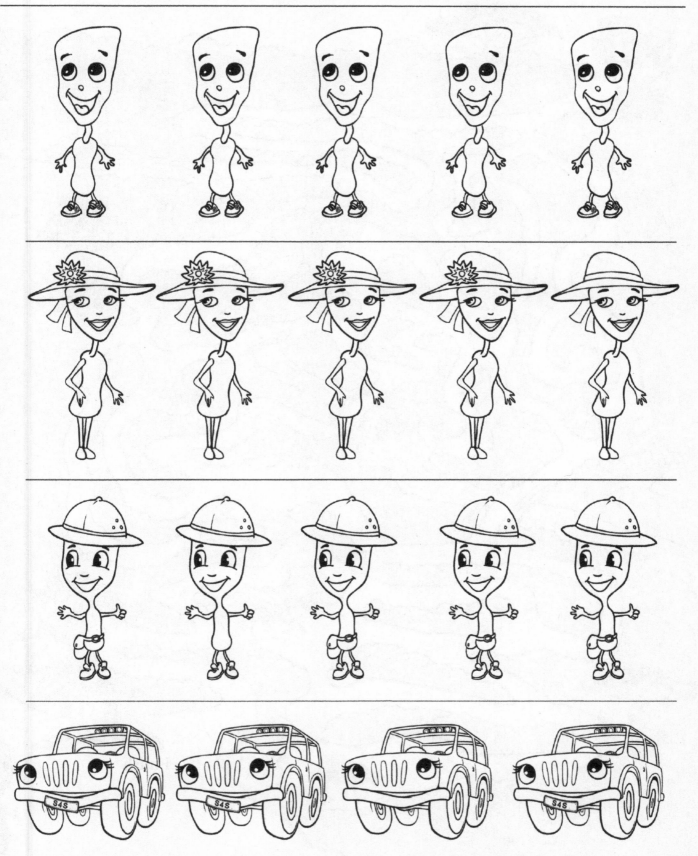

QUICKLY's Safari Maze

Travel through the Safari Maze with Quickly.

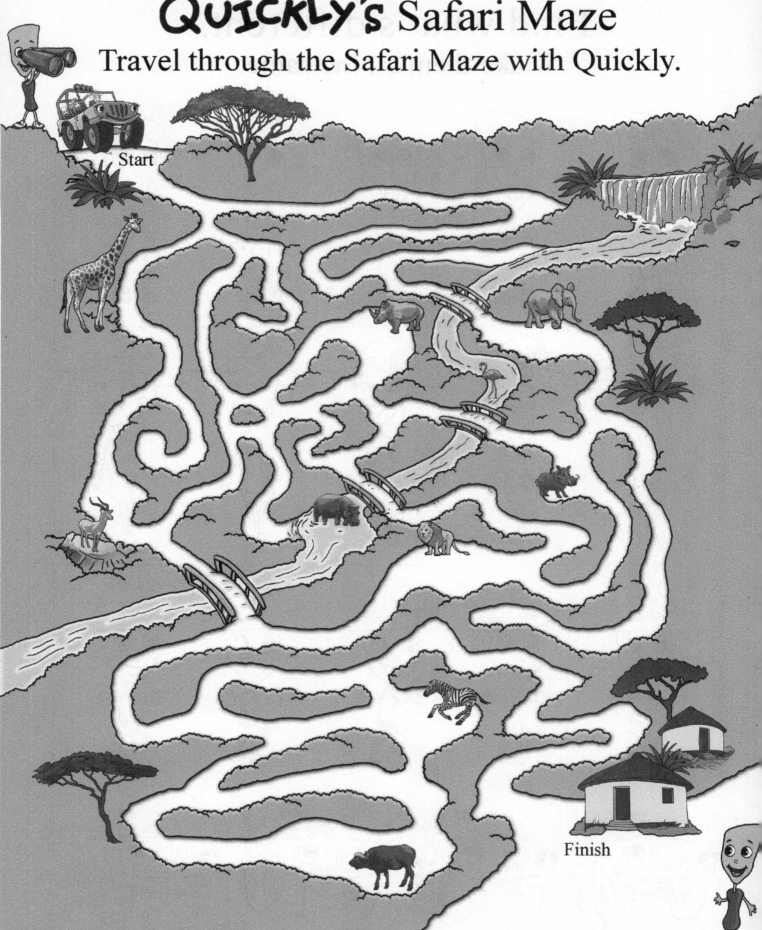

Start

Finish

Color The Big Five

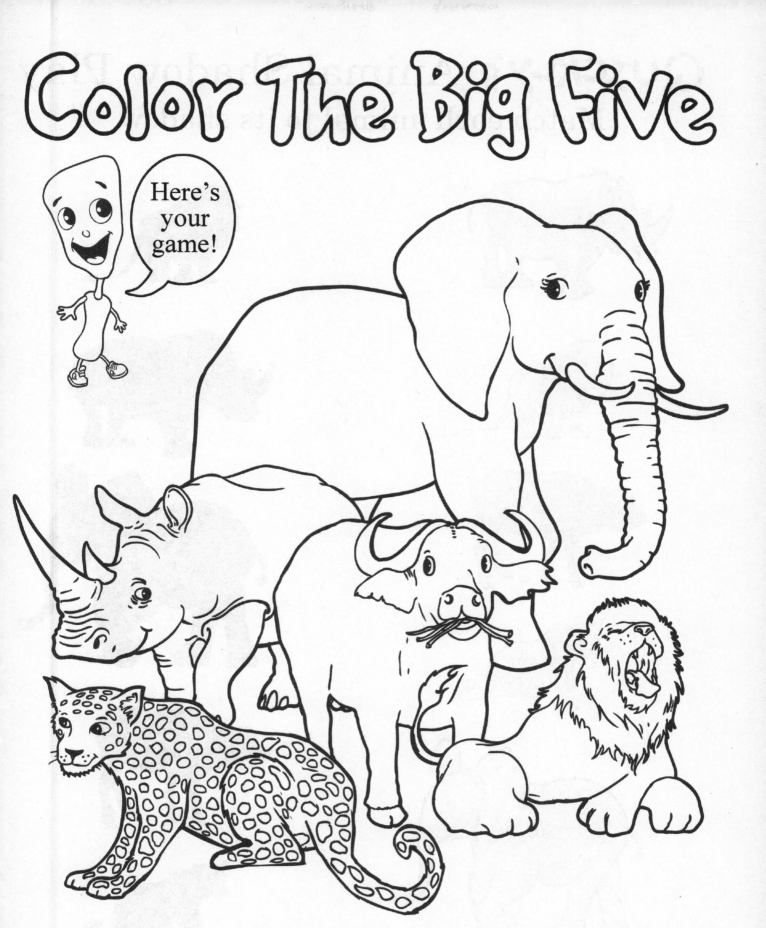

Here's your game!

Can you say their names?

QUICKLY's Animal Shadow Play
Match each animal to its shadow.

Draw your favorite animal.

Color the Hidden Picture.

1 - blue   2 - gray   3 - brown   4 - white

Connect the Dots.

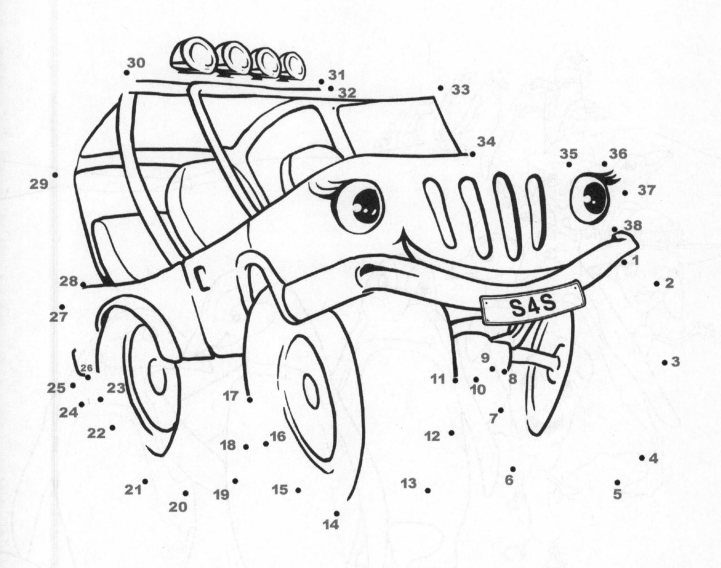

Color
PanDora, QUICKLY, and Ponnie.

Color the Hidden Picture.

1 - red   2 - gray   3 - blue   4 - white

QUICKLY's Wordsearch

Help Quickly find his words.

```
Q K P A N D O R A S O G V F L
U E A K I Y L L P X P H V N E
I I N G T Y N A Y L O C I U O
C K C I A A T I U A N Q S M P
K I A R E L I O N F N U A X A
L V K A L D D X O I I G Q C R
Y B E F N I Y P L L E J N P D
C U S F L O A L H D D S W G B
E F L E S R H I N O C E R O S
Y F Y X L W H A A G Q W R A R
I A Y L U P A N C A K E S N H
N L J Q L K W B R K X Z A K A
L O E S U E L E P H A N T B F
B V Z Q E D T N D X F Y Y Q X
```

LION	GIRAFFE
BUFFALO	PONNIE
RHINOCEROS	PANDORA
LEOPARD	QUICKLY
ELEPHANT	PANCAKES

44

QUICKLY's Animal Shadow Play
Match each animal to its shadow.

This is your page!

QUICKLY'S
next adventure

will be
out of
this world!

More Fun with QUICKLY

Read Quickly's adventures with your friends.

Look for:

QUICKLY
THE MAGIC SPATULA

QUICKLY'S
MAGICAL PANCAKE ADVENTURE

S is for Safari
An Alphabetical Adventure
with
QUICKLY
THE MAGIC SPATULA